LIBRA

HOROSCOPE

& ASTROLOGY

2022

Published by Mystic Cat Press

Suite SM-2380-6403

14601 North Bybee Lake Court

Portland, Oregon 97203

Phone: +1 (805) 308-6503

SiaSands@hotmail.com

Copyright © 2021 by Mystic Cat Press

Contents

LIBRA 2022
HOROSCOPE & ASTROLOGY

Four Weeks Per Month

Week 1 – Days 1 - 7

Week 2 – Days 8 - 14

Week 3 – Days 15 - 21

Week 4 – Days 22 – Month-end

LIBRA

Libra Dates: September 23rd to October 22nd
Symbol: Scales
Element: Air
Planet: Venus
House: Seventh
Colors: Ivory, pink, light-blue

2022 AT A GLANCE

Eclipses

Partial Solar – April 30th

Total Lunar – May 16th

Partial Solar – October 25th

Total Lunar -November 8th

Equinoxes and Solstices

Spring - March 20th

Summer - June 21st

Fall – September 23rd

Winter – December 21st

Mercury Retrogrades

January 14th, Aquarius - February 4th Capricorn

May 10th, Gemini - June 3rd, Taurus

September 10th, Libra - October 2nd Virgo

December 29th, Capricorn - January 1st, 2023, Capricorn

2022 FULL MOONS

Wolf Moon: January 17th, 23:48.

Snow Moon: February 16th, 16:57

Worm Moon March 18th, 07:17

Pink Moon: April 16th, 18:54

Flower Moon: May 16th, 04:13

Strawberry Moon: June 14th, 11:51

Buck Moon: July 13th, 18:37

Sturgeon Moon: August 12th, 01:35

Corn, Harvest Moon: September 10th, 09:59

Hunters Moon: October 9th, 20:54

Beaver Moon: November 8th, 11:01

Cold Moon: December 8th, 04:07

THE MOON PHASES

🌑 New Moon (Dark Moon)

🌒 Waxing Crescent Moon

🌓 First Quarter Moon

🌔 Waxing Gibbous Moon

🌕 Full Moon

🌖 Waning Gibbous (Disseminating) Moon

🌗 Third (Last/Reconciling) Quarter Moon

🌘 Waning Crescent (Balsamic) Moon

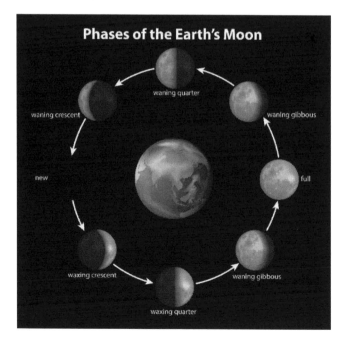

Phases of the Earth's Moon

2022

JANUARY
M	T	W	T	F	S	S
					1	2
3	4	5	6	7	8	9
10	11	12	13	14	15	16
17	18	19	20	21	22	23
24	25	26	27	28	29	30
31						

FEBRUARY
M	T	W	T	F	S	S
	1	2	3	4	5	6
9	10	11	12	11	12	13
14	15	16	17	18	19	20
21	22	23	24	25	26	27
28						

MARCH
M	T	W	T	F	S	S
	1	2	3	4	4	6
7	8	9	10	11	12	13
14	15	16	17	18	19	20
21	22	23	24	25	26	27
28	29	30	31			

APRIL
M	T	W	T	F	S	S
				1	2	3
4	5	6	7	8	9	10
11	12	13	14	15	16	17
18	19	20	21	22	23	24
25	26	27	28	29	30	

MAY
M	T	W	T	F	S	S
						1
2	3	4	5	6	7	8
9	10	11	12	13	14	15
16	17	18	19	20	21	22
23	24	25	26	27	28	29
30	31					

JUNE
M	T	W	T	F	S	S
	1	2	3	4	5	
6	7	8	9	10	11	12
13	14	15	16	17	18	19
20	21	22	23	24	25	26
27	28	29	30			

JULY
M	T	W	T	F	S	S
				1	2	3
4	5	6	7	8	9	10
11	12	13	14	15	16	17
18	19	20	21	22	23	24
25	26	27	28	29	30	31

AUGUST
M	T	W	T	F	S	S
1	2	3	4	5	6	7
8	9	10	11	12	13	14
15	16	17	18	19	20	21
22	23	24	25	26	27	28
29	30	31				

SEPTEMBER
M	T	W	T	F	S	S
			1	2	3	4
5	6	7	8	9	10	11
12	13	14	15	16	17	18
19	20	21	22	23	24	25
26	27	28	29	30		

OCTOBER
M	T	W	T	F	S	S
					1	2
3	4	5	6	7	8	9
10	11	12	13	14	15	16
17	18	19	20	21	22	23
24	25	26	27	28	29	30
31						

NOVEMBER
M	T	W	T	F	S	S
	1	2	3	4	5	6
7	8	9	10	11	12	13
14	15	16	17	18	19	20
21	22	23	24	25	26	27
28	29	30				

DECEMBER
M	T	W	T	F	S	S
			1	2	3	4
5	6	7	8	9	10	11
12	13	14	15	16	17	18
19	20	21	22	23	24	25
26	27	28	29	30	31	

Time set to Coordinated Universal Time Zone

(UT±0)

Meteor Showers are on the date they peak.

JANUARY

Sun	Mon	Tue	Wed	Thu	Fri	Sat
						1
2	3	4	5	6	7	8
9	10	11	12	13	14	15
16	17	18	19	20	21	22
23	24	25	26	27	28	29
30	31					

January 2nd - New Moon in Capricorn 18:33

January 3rd - Quadrantids Meteor Shower. January 1st-5th.

January 7th - Mercury at Greatest Eastern Elongation

January 9th - First Quarter Moon in Aries 18:11

January 14th - Mercury Retrograde begins in Aquarius

January 17th - Wolf Moon. Full Moon in Cancer 23:48

January 25th - Last Quarter Moon Scorpio 13:42

FULL MOON

The Quadrantids Meteor Shower blazes across the night sky, illuminating remarkable potential this week. You are ready for a new chapter, and it's likely to revitalize your life with refreshing options. It brings a social environment that widens your social circle with a sense of support, connection, and companionship. A spontaneous decision provides a dash of adventure. You blend raw ingredients to come up with ample opportunities to improve your situation. It offers a chance to develop a bond, and sharing thoughts with this person draws excitement. It opens the floodgates to new possibilities that light up the areas of inspiration and joy.

Nurturing your dreams draws a pleasing result. It stirs energy of manifestation that opens the path ahead. It sets the tone to discover a journey that speaks to your heart. It connects you with like-minded people, and this weeds out the problematic areas. Social interaction is a valuable tool that draws sustenance into your environment.

A new option is arriving soon. It opens a compelling road that allows you to break free of constraints and set forth on a new adventure. It gives you the green light to get involved with a community endeavor. There is a surprise nestles ahead that draws social engagement. It is an aspect that soothes nerves as it brings a calming influence into your life. It has a grounding effect that builds stable foundations.

Mercury Retrograde begins in Aquarius at the week's end. Downtime is needed to process emotions as the Mercury Retrograde phase is a difficult chapter. It's not an easy time. Still, as you move forward, flexibility and adaptability will help you navigate around any bumps in the road. Some news is coming that brings excitement; it removes limiting beliefs around security. It opens the floodgates to an enterprising avenue forward. It brings an active and productive chapter of working towards your vision. It gets a chance to branch out and grow your talents.

Keeping an eye for new options paints a broader picture of what is possible. It draws a curious chapter that offers unique experiences. There are a few twists and turns as you navigate forward. It brings a time of chasing your dream and developing a plan that captures the essence of wanderlust. Change is part of this process, and it has the potential to reinvent your world from the ground up. A slower pace helps integrate these changes as you journey towards abundance. Acting on your instincts helps unearth options that grow your talents. News arrives that brings an optimistic tone into your life. It helps you sidestep roadblocks and open a path that progresses life forward. Staying open to new possibilities brings options that grow your talents. Creativity is heightening, bringing side options to explore. An abundant mindset lets you unearth a unique trail forward. A little worn path enables you to research a side journey that is good for your soul.

The Wolf Moon. Full Moon in Cancer this week is a new chapter on many levels. A time of rejuvenation is approaching. It helps you move away from issues and release troublesome energy. Shaking off the heavy vibes opens a fresh start that lets you move ahead with purposefulness. It turns the page on a new chapter that is instrumental in improving the prospects in your world. You transition towards abundance, and it lets you tap into the potential that soothes the frayed edges. It enables you to join forces with another who brings the gift of companionship into your world. It opens the gate to new possibilities that inspire growth.

The Full Moon energy centers around stability and security. Pressure eases, reducing stress. It translates into a chapter where you can focus on projects and ventures that make the most of your creativity. Dabbling in your interests draws balance and abundance into your surroundings. It drives communication with friends that offer collaboration, growth, and kingship. It's a refreshing change as drama sweeps out to sea, and you can set sail on a new adventure that captures your interest. Opportunities ahead help improve security in your life. You create a stable foundation that leads to a chapter of progressing goals. New ideas and options provide a refreshing environment that inspires and offers a chance for collaboration. A side journey beckons; using your talents and exploring the possibilities open a wellspring of options that leave you feeling optimistic.

Things are on the move for your social life soon. An exciting aspect flows into your world and lightens the atmosphere. You connect with those out of touch, which paves the way forward towards a more lively environment. Entertaining and connecting with your tribe is a theme that resonates abundance. It gets the ball rolling on an enriching phase of expansion that sees a personal goal taking shape. Remember, when you lay your bets via your intuition, things soon fall into place, drawing a pleasing result.

Taking inventories of your situation helps you pinpoint the areas best removed. It streamlines effectively and lets you focus on the avenues that offer the highest reward. It helps bridge the gap between your current situation and your future aspirations. It's an excellent time to upgrade dreams and plot a course towards future growth. A process of tearing down outworn energy reveals new possibilities ready to blossom. Lovely changes ahead bring happiness flowing into your world. Immersing yourself in a new project draws a time of heightened creativity.

An option arrives that helps you push back barriers and create a bridge to a lighter chapter. It marks the start of something big as it brings new pathways that grow your world. An optimistic mindset cultivates flexibility, and this lets you adeptly navigate a complex environment as you move forward towards expansion.

FEBRUARY

Sun	Mon	Tue	Wed	Thu	Fri	Sat
		1	2	3	4	5
6	7	8	9	10	11	12
13	14	15	16	17	18	19
20	21	22	23	24	25	26
27	28					

February 1st - New Moon in Aquarius 05:45
February 1st - Chinese New Year (Tiger)
February 1st - Imbolc

February 4th - Mercury Retrograde ends in Capricorn

February 8th - First Quarter Moon in Taurus 13:50

February 16th - Mercury at Greatest Western Elongation
February 16th - Snow Moon. Full Moon in Leo 16:57

February 23rd - Last Quarter Moon in Scorpio 22:32

NEW MOON

FULL MOON

A new page of life is ready to open, and you benefit from events on the horizon. It brings a refreshing change of pace that opens the gateway towards growth and expansion. It leads to developments and new potential around your social life that draws an engaging chapter of harmonizing interpersonal bonds—connecting with friends earmarks a time of happiness ahead. A freedom-driven time makes the most of your rebellious energy; it draws positive results that release the pressure. You fling open the window to a fresh start and enjoy sunny skies overhead. It brings a boost to confidence and happiness.

A refreshing change is coming that opens heighten potential in your social life. It has you exploring possibilities with an engaging companion. It brings an optimistic phase that lets you make headway on planning for future growth. It ignites a bond that gets you involved in lively discussions. It releases the heaviness and helps you embrace nurturing a situation that offers lighter energy. It stirs up the heartwarming time that enriches your world. It brings excitement to the forefront of your life. Change is imminent. It flings open the doors, and a cascade of new possibilities arrive to get the ball rolling on developing an extraordinary chapter forward. It brings a rhythm that is active, dynamic, and inspired. You may notice a commutative element in the air as people reach out and sync up with you. It brings social engagement and a lively atmosphere.

There is an improvement coming around home and family life. You land in a stable environment ripe for growth. It lets you set off on a new adventure; it delivers a happy and progressive phase. It brings a time that rules expansion, which begins a positive trend that flows through your world. It connects with an aspect of personal growth that puts you in contact with like-minded individuals. Using technology to your advantage, you maintain bonds that grow your social life.

You are doing the right thing by expanding your life. It does take you out of your comfort zone, but the results are pleasing. It offers security, abundance, and joy. A lighter chapter is coming that sets your heart ablaze with inspiration. Taking time to nurture this energy gently draws sunny skies overhead. A clear path opens that brings new joy into your personal life. It creates a strong foundation that offers room to progress.

An important decision is cropping up in your life soon. It speaks of a vital shift occurring that brings expansion. It links you up to a new chapter that enables you to circulate and enjoy the sunshine overhead. It does bring social options that help you gain traction on expanding your social life. You enjoy sharing time with a valued companion this week.

The Full Moon in Leo this week does wipe the slate clean on many levels. There may be a sense of uncertainty holding you back. A time of self-discovery and contemplation brings the answers needed to move forward towards change. It initiates a stable phase of growth that opens the floodgates to a happy chapter. Harnessing the magic in your life lets you use the power of your creativity to come up with viable options worth developing. A lead ahead brings movement and discovery.

News arrives that brings a burst of inspiration and opportunity. It breathes life into your surroundings and provides an avenue to grow your talents. Gifts of creativity that are currently dormant soon flourish under a prosperous sky. It drives the freedom-loving chapter that liberates your mood and offers an influx of options to tempt you towards growth. Manifestation gently flows through your life, bringing the correct path forward.

It shows a time of personal growth ahead that draws soul-expanding experiences. It provides insight and clarity into the direction onward. Indeed, something inspirational flows into your world and gives you plenty of smiles. It touches you down on a chapter that offers change and growth. It brings ample time for transformation and new adventures. Making yourself a priority is essential.

Your career path ahead is to an upswing. Life brings opportunities to unpack and explore. It sets a refreshing trend that offers room to grow your skills by dabbling in a side hustle. The seeds you plant marks a new beginning that help develop a prosperous working life. A venture takes shape and begins to branch out into new areas. Feedback and guidance helped guide the path ahead. Reevaluating progress helps sidestep potential hurdles and bring faster progression to light.

Opportunities on the horizon offer swift progress. It activates a sense of adventure and excitement when something new tempts you forward. It brings a rewarding time that opens pathways of creativity and self-expression. Being receptive to change offers options for growth, learning, and advancement. It triggers a cascade of possibilities that grow your talents, and this heightens potential.

Life brings opportunities that help in many ways. It lets you spread your wings and soar to great heights as a new adventure comes calling. It lights a path of valuable growth that enables you to maneuver forward and embrace developing your vision. A lovely perk arrives, and this encourages a shift forward that has you exploring a journey that makes your heart sing. It turns the leaf on a new chapter that draws abundance.

MARCH

Sun	Mon	Tue	Wed	Thu	Fri	Sat
		1	2	3	4	5
6	7	8	9	10	11	12
13	14	15	16	17	18	19
20	21	22	23	24	25	26
27	28	29	30	31		

March 2nd - New Moon in Pisces 17:34

March 10th - First Quarter Moon in Gemini 10:45

March 18th - Worm Moon. Full Moon in Virgo 07:17

March 20th - Ostara/Spring Equinox 15:33

March 25th - Last Quarter Moon in Capricorn 05:37

FULL MOON

New Moon in Pisces reveals a new undercurrent of potential that surrounds your life. It is the right time to create a vision board and put various options out there to contemplate. After a time of soul-searching, you touch down a path that highlights new possibilities—getting involved in advancing your abilities dials up your unique brand of wisdom and knowledge. It puts the shine on advancing your abilities and extending your reach into new areas. It draws a busy time that offers news and information.

A business idea takes off and blossoms into a venture worth developing. Soon enough, you see positive signs that feel encouraging. It focuses on expansion as it cracks the code to a well-designed journey that supports well-being and growth. It increases optimism and improves your life by letting you reshape goals and plot a course towards advancement. Wisely investing your time draws dividends.

Change surrounds your life; being open to something new kicks off a chapter of possibilities. It marks the start of a fun and vibrant phase of exploring the synergy with a unique character. Opportunities to mingle encourage a degree of expansion that shapes the path ahead. It offers a rich time of sharing thoughts and discussing items of interest with someone who inspires personal growth.

It's an excellent time to explore new horizons as things are on the move in your life. It brings communication that highlights a path forward. It connects you with a refreshing social aspect that puts you in touch with kindred spirits. It translates to an abundant chapter ahead that brings lighter energy into your world. Sharing thoughts and ideas during this time reverberate around your life in a widening circle of abundance.

Exciting new options flow in to inspire growth. It lifts troubles; the path ahead shifts and lightens. It brings the gift of expansion, activity, and inspiration. It all helps banish negativity and release outworn areas that limit progress. Being proactive advances your vision as you begin building rock-solid foundations. It brings a new start that lets you gain momentum on improving your circumstances.

You unlock the key to an essential time of growing your world in a new direction. A flash of insight and creativity directs your attention towards a refreshing option that takes you on a new journey forward. It lets you forge ahead as you discover a route that takes courage but offers advancement. Growing and evolving your talents enables you to tap into incredible results. A willingness to try new endeavors lets in the goodness. You can set your sights on a long-term goal and know things are coming together nicely. It offers a social environment that draws pathways that take you towards personal growth.

A Full Moon in Virgo this week. At the end of the week, Ostara/Spring Equinox brings the Sun again after the long winter. A path of higher wisdom and learning comes calling. It illuminates change and brings options to develop a journey that speaks to your heart. A new source of prosperity flows into your life, drawing stability. It lets you use your talents and gifts to elevate the potential in your world. You land in an environment ripe for progression. It helps you navigate a complicated time and come out the other side more resilient. Life-affirming possibilities connect you with the tribe of kindred spirits, which lays the groundwork for a web of support.

Something percolating in the background soon appears miraculously. It brings a boost that lets you combine your skills with a dream option. Tackling a new project emphasizes improving your life; it drives a purposeful and active path forward. A change ahead sets your life ablaze with new possibilities. It opens a gateway towards growth. Being receptive and open to change lets you flex your adaptability and shine.

It speaks of an exciting possibility that makes the dashing entrance into your life soon. It heightens your sense of purpose; it brings new options that capitalize on your talents. A chance to flex your abilities is nourishment for your spirit. It lets you negotiate a tricky environment and move towards calmer waters. It draws a social environment that links you with kindred spirits.

Alchemy is brewing in the background of your life that suggests new options arrive soon. It has you entering a prosperous cycle and does let you make a creative mark on the path ahead. New potential and a fresh outlook ahead draw dividends. It connects you to magic and possibility. Expanding your life lets you uncover a little nugget of gold worth exploring. You set sail on a voyage that offers happiness and abundance. It emphasizes growth, advancement, and prosperity. Nurturing your environment lets you branch out and extend your talents into new areas. A passage forward opens, and this marks the beginning of an emotional journey. Life moves from strength to strength as you become adept at navigating in a changing environment. You can grow by leaps and bounds by expanding your horizons and taking a leap of faith towards learning a new ability.

There is a passion path that brings a bonus into your life. You also find luck and inspiration are your partners in crime on this journey towards developing your life. You can make gains by gathering wisdom and weaving a basket of success. You hit a home run and taste the sweet nectar of success when you embark on an enterprising chapter. There is good news coming; you won't encounter delays or roadblocks ahead. You are ready to make progress and forge a way to achieve a robust result. Advancement is going to play a prominent aspect over the next time.

APRIL

Sun	Mon	Tue	Wed	Thu	Fri	Sat
					1	2
3	4	5	6	7	8	9
10	11	12	13	14	15	16
17	18	19	20	21	22	23
24	25	26	27	28	29	30

April 1st - New Moon in Aries 06:24

April 9th - First Quarter Moon in Cancer 06:47

April 16th - Pink Moon. Full Moon in Libra 18:54

April 22nd - Lyrids Meteor Shower from April 16-25

April 23rd - Last Quarter Moon in Aquarius 11:56.

April 29th - Mercury Greatest Eastern Elongation of 20.6 degrees from the Sun.

April 30th - New Moon in Taurus 20:27

NEW MOON

FULL MOON

New Moon in Aries this week gives the green light to move forward towards developing an area of interest. A life-changing chapter ahead creates a flurry of excitement when a new role emerges. You gain a glimpse of glittering possibilities and soon thrive in a busy and active environment. An area that has been on the backburner for a while gets the shift forward. It helps you sort out and organize the aspects of your life that had become disruptive. Streamlining and juggling demands draws the essence of efficiency to progress your life forward effectively. A powerful influence flows into your world, setting the stage for an enterprising chapter of growth.

News arrives, which offers a chance to follow your passion. It takes your focus off the beaten track when you discover an enticing side journey that gives room to grow your abilities in a new direction. You enter a phase of learning and guidance that shapes the path ahead. It ushers in new energy that has you thinking about the possibilities. It inspires a stage of working towards a fixed goal. Expanding your life leads to a memorable phase that creates positive change. It lets you harness the power of your creativity and embrace an adventurous time of expansion. Life opens to a new flavor that enables you to reach for more. An opportunity comes knocking; it creates space to chase a dream. As you take those first tentative steps to improve your situation, information arrives; it lets you hit your stride and progress forward.

The goodness and joy flow into your life when information reaches you, sparks a new chapter. News arrives that hits the sweet spot. It brings a lighter chapter that draws abundance and excitement into your world. New options pave the way forward for progress to occur. You reveal an avenue that offers growth, productivity, and expansion. It lets you dive into developing an area that provides room to expand horizons and heighten your career potential. A side trail soon blossoms.

You gather the assistance of someone effective in evaluating ideas and offering advice. It brings a time of brainstorming sessions that see innovative solutions rising. It brings a burst of inspiration to your creative process. It delivers results and offers room to advance your situation forward. Cultivating your gifts unearths advancement that takes your abilities towards a lofty goal. It lights a passage towards improving your circumstances that draw well-being and abundance.

It is a time that sees you become more expressive about what you seek in life. Indeed, life blossoms under your willingness to explore new possibilities. You discover a vocation that grows your abilities, and this lets you shine brightly. It ramps up the potential possible and brings a phase of working with your creativity to achieve new growth.

There is incoming potential likely to surge in your social life. You thread a sense of joy through keeping connected with loved ones. While things have been quiet on the social front, it soon brings ripeness into your life with new options ahead that draw social engagement. It marks a new beginning that opens a fresh chapter. You reawaken to the potential possible in your extended social circle. Communication arrives that has you seeing your circle of friends in a new light.

Gifts and lessons weave throughout your situation. You have increased your knowledge base and improved your position by utilizing lessons learned to overcome trials and hurdles. You soon become grounded in new responsibilities when news arrives that brings enterprising information to your door. Something new is on offer, and this lets you navigate the path forward towards a pleasing outcome. Curiosity and creativity heighten as you unearth a lead that offers room to progress your talents. Exploring the options connects you with characters who have similar interests.

It is a time that marks a significant improvement as it transitions you towards new possibilities that encourage growth and learning. Being open to change room lifts the lid on new opportunities that inspire an engaging journey. It brings a rich landscape that awakens a sense of adventure.

Lyrids Meteor Shower brings a powerhouse of fresh energy into your environment. Surprise news brings tremendous changes to your home life. You move forward with a clear head that enables progress to occur. Taking care of business, you soon get cracking on developing your vision. Honing in on your true purpose marks a necessary time of transition that sees elevated potential flowing into your world. Using the energy of manifestation lets you fast-track a cycle of growth.

This surprise hits the right note. It reveals itself quickly when information arrives that encourages change. It draws an enlightening perspective that gives you a fresh outlook about the path ahead. More surprises are on the horizon, bringing messages and opportunities. It marks an expressive and social chapter that puts the shine on your personal life. It helps you evaluate goals and lets you figure out new areas of personal growth and self-development.

You can expect a few twists and turns this week. It opens a chapter of discovery that lets you build a bridge towards a brighter future. You invest your time in developing an area that shows promise. It brings a project that becomes a jewel in your crown. The potential for success moves forward in leaps and bounds. It links up to positive change that draws blessings in your world.

MAY

Sun	Mon	Tue	Wed	Thu	Fri	Sat
1	2	3	4	5	6	7
8	9	10	11	12	13	14
15	16	17	18	19	20	21
22	23	24	25	26	27	28
29	30	31				

May 6th - Eta Aquarids Meteor Shower, April 19th - May 28th

May 9th - First Quarter Moon in Leo 00:21

May 10th - Mercury Retrograde begins in Gemini

May 16th - Total Lunar Eclipse 01:32

May 16th - Flower Moon. Full Moon in Scorpio 04:13

May 22nd - Last Quarter Moon in Aquarius 18:43

May - 30th - New Moon in Leo 00:21

Eta Aquarids Meteor Shower brings an opportunity to broaden your vision; it brings a time of expansion, freedom, and optimism. An enterprising area gets a chance to rebrand your image. It grows your talents and harnesses creative thinking to set your sights higher. You raise the bar and learn an area that increases your knowledge and heightens your abilities. It gives you a chance to build a site that brings new possibilities into your environment. As you move forward towards advancing to the next level, you reshape goals and revolutionize the potential possible in your world. Ramping up the success rate brings momentum that offers progress.

It brings a turning point that sweeps in change. It lets you embrace a lighter aspect that brings an active and open chapter. It earmarks a new beginning that redefines the path ahead. It enables you to move away from drama and open your life to the right kind of friendships. It brings people closer and draws a valuable sense of connection. It's a landscape ripe with possibility. It brings a companion who offers insight and advice. It brings a burst of sunshine into your world. A little worn path opens to tempt growth. It provides diversity, expansion, and advancement. Once you ignite curiosity, little hold you back from growing a new interest. It becomes an excellent side hobby that draws a financial benefit.

Mercury retrograde causes mayhem and disruption in your social life when it begins in Gemini this week. Open communication smooths out any bumps that may threaten to derail progress. It helps you develop a path towards your dreams. Focusing on nurturing an important bond lets you forge ahead and take in the planning of lofty goals. A strong emphasis on improving your home environment cultivates fresh energy that breaks up stagnant patterns. It heightens the potential in your social life, bringing a boost into your world.

Being selective raises the bar. It helps distance from limiting areas that drain your enthusiasm. Be proactive about setting barriers as appropriate. Soul-searching draws clarity; it brings insight into the path ahead. A diverse track opens that brings unique characters into your life, which lays the groundwork for expansion. It brings an influx of potential that offers time to nurture abilities. Change surrounds your life; a myriad of possibilities tempt you forward. It brings you in contact with a kindred spirit who offers insightful advice.

Stabilizing your foundations brings a suitable climate to see past struggles fade away. It's best to place troubled energy in the rear vision mirror. As you shift your focus forward, new areas tempt you towards growth. Streamlining and refining your vision draws a flow of new possibilities. It puts you in the correct alignment to make the most of your talents.

Flower Moon. Full Moon in Scorpio brings insight into an interpersonal bond that had been feeling out of balance recently. Communication ahead lets you navigate a complex environment and improve the potential possible. It allows you to swim upstream towards smoother waters that draw stability. Information forward provides insight that lets you see your situation; differently; it links you to a social aspect that draws harmony. It emphasizes improving a connection with someone who opens their heart and shares their secrets with you.

Indeed, new potential flows into your social life. A better cast of characters emerges, and this draws light and positive energy into your world. Certainly, staying open to new possibilities lights a path of increasing optimism. It brings a lively time of social engagement and exciting conversations. Someone with a link to your past bridges the gap to catch up on the news.

Life reveals a curious twist that brings developments in your personal life. You discover fun and adventurous times that align your heart closer to a charismatic character who resonates a charming aspect. Sharing ideas and thoughts with another brings support and guidance that lights the path forward. Strong potential in your social life brings the type of personal expansion that is so valuable.

A New Moon in Leo is a great time to set aspirations and intentions for the month ahead. You can embrace developing goals as improvement looms overhead. A creative aspect brings the start of an exciting endeavor that gives you solid footing on progressing your talents. It takes your abilities further and draws a new role that grows your skills. Life holds a refreshing change, and this brings happiness to your table. It helps you make tracks to improving your circumstances. Reshaping goals initiates transformation.

Life attracts a new array of possibilities. Friends seek you out; social engagement is on the rise. It brings an interest in new areas and offers pathways towards growth. It leads to a richly creative and expressive environment that draws a pleasing result. It sets up a stable foundation that helps progress your situation outwardly. You navigate the complexities with grace and resilience. Changes ahead rejuvenate and renew your energy, bringing new options to explore. A journey of adventure and discovery tempt you forward.

It speaks of a shift forward that inspires. It clears away limitations and lets you head towards new possibilities. It offers a solid foundation that draws security into your home life. Fanning the fires of inspiration, you discover an open road of exciting options that tempts you forward. New characters expand your social life, drawing a valuable sense of connection.

JUNE

Sun	Mon	Tue	Wed	Thu	Fri	Sat
			1	2	3	4
5	6	7	8	9	10	11
12	13	14	15	16	17	18
19	20	21	22	23	24	25
26	27	28	29	30		

June 3rd - Mercury Retrograde ends in Taurus

June 7th - First Quarter Moon in Virgo 14:48

June 14th - Strawberry Moon. Full Moon in Sagittarius Supermoon 11:51

June 16th - Mercury's greatest Western elongation of 23.2 degrees from the Sun

June 21st - Last Quarter Moon in Aries 03:11

June 21st - Midsummer/Litha Solstice 09:13

June 29th - New Moon in Cancer 02:52

FULL MOON

Mercury Retrograde ends in Taurus. It gives you a private picture of what is possible in your social life. It lets you embark on developing a situation that becomes close to your heart. Communication flows into your world that brings expansion and adds an exciting flavor to your life. It sees ideas shared and possibilities bounced around with someone who captures your interest. It brings a busy and productive time that places a focus on deepening interpersonal bonds. It heightens confidence and offers room to progress your life forward.

You are ready to improve your bottom line and soon set off on developing a lofty goal. Life picks up steam, and new possibilities offer dynamic potential that brings the room to grow your talents. A magic option lets you create space to nurture creativity by getting involved in a new area. It brings a foundation that offers a stable basis to journey towards growth. The right conditions expand options, and this hits a sweet note.

You link up with a person who helps you move away from sadness. Any outworn energy hanging around the situation is soon released. It brings a time of nurturing a bond that offers impressive results. It draws an active time of growing the possibilities with this person. Positive change ahead fuels your desire to adapt and grow. It connects you with a like-minded individual.

The Full Moon in Sagittarius Supermoon at week's end brings a curious benefit. You find peace by creating a sanctuary around your home life. It plants the seeds that draw stability and balance into your immediate environment. It also lets you continue to expand your life by initiating new projects. Indeed, events on the horizon tempt you forward and encourage you to engage in developing goals. It draws a gentle element that offers enriching rewards. It brings a social aspect that sends ripples of abundance throughout your life. It nourishes your world and connects you with others who provide support.

Small changes create extensive pathways towards growth. As you broaden your horizons, you enjoy a light-hearted chapter that develops your skills. It brings a social aspect that offers room to mingle with like-minded characters. Dreams take flight, bringing renewal to your door. Making your vision a priority draws momentum and progress. Old challenges melt away, and an emphasis on security draws a stable foundation. It sees improvement is occurring in areas of friendship, social engagement, and networking. It brings laughter and liveness into your social life.

As your life expands outwardly, you discover new friends and companions. You enter a social aspect that grows your world and brings a breakthrough moment you can treasure. You reveal an admirer who has a flair for making you happy.

Midsummer/Litha Solstice at week's end is an ideal time to reflect on your goals. You explore a spiritual path that heightens your abilities. It allows room to evolve into a new pathway of growth and learning. It brings a journey that is inspiring, trailblazing, and eclectic. Life gets a reboot, taking you towards a chapter of nurturing your talents. Being flexible opens the floodgates to grounding energy that restores balance.

A lovely time ahead that hits a high note in your social life. It helps you clear away limitations and expand horizons by engaging more in your community. It brings a positive outlook that ignites your imagination with fresh inspiration. It draws the correct characters into your life. It aligns you with a time of heightened activity and lively discussions. It brings sunny skies overhead as you focus on an area that holds meaning. Improving your circumstances helps you create a breakthrough that takes you towards a happier chapter. You have earned the right to nurture your life. New energy flows into your world that brings rejuvenation. A blank canvas of possibilities tempts you forward. Time spent on the home front draws abundance and invites new pathways towards growth. It opens a creative aspect that grows your world by being open to learning areas and working with your talents. It places you in the prime alignment to solidify foundations and draw equilibrium into your home life. A prominent area of your energy comes calling, bringing the new potential to light.

The New Moon in Cancer gets a new role opening, bringing a cutting-edge environment that offers room to grow your career path. It takes advantage of innovative technology and brings new possibilities to your door. It lets you make a decisive move that helps you power ahead. Your working environment expands as you launch into a new chapter of big plans. You fuel inspiration with newfound motivation. It brings advancement to your working life. A goal comes to life that sparks a shift forward. Your gifts are growing, and you are likely to seek out like-minded people to connect with a diverse tribe of kindred spirits.

Something is on offer for your life soon. It brings a journey towards happiness and harmony. It lets you negotiate complexities and reach an environment that carries you forward. A transition comes calling that encourages learning a new area. It gives you a chance to develop your skills and advance your abilities.

You discover that things come together, serendipitously. It brings clear skies overhead that nurture your spirit by expanding your social life. It creates the change that offers room to move in alignment with a long-held vision. You seal the deal by being open and nurturing the potential possible. Stability and security are the focal points that drive this situation forward. Growing your social life brings foundations that are balanced and able to expand outwardly.

JULY

Sun	Mon	Tue	Wed	Thu	Fri	Sat
					1	2
3	4	5	6	7	8	9
10	11	12	13	14	15	16
17	18	19	20	21	22	23
24	25	26	27	28	29	30
31						

July 7th - First Quarter Moon in Libra 02:14

July 13th - Buck Moon. Full Moon in Capricorn. Supermoon 18:37

July 20th - Last Quarter Moon in Aries 14:18

July 28th - New Moon in Leo 17:54

July 28th - Delta Aquarids Meteor Shower. July 12th - August 23rd

FULL MOON

There is plenty to stoke the fires of your inspiration. You breeze through an auspicious chapter that grows your abilities, and it takes your ambitions to the next level. It triggers a path that sees new possibilities emerging in your career that tempt you towards advancement. It highlights a chapter of abundance that is the result of your willingness to open to new opportunities. Raising the bar high, let you pursue a lofty goal.

Changes ahead create a growth-orientated environment. It lets you move forward in a sustainable and balanced manner. Adjusting to the changes ahead takes flexibility, but you are more adept at navigating a complex environment. It takes you towards achieving structure and stability. Changes in the wind, transformation flows into your world as a new trajectory is possible. Imagination and creative thinking heighten, letting you come up with trailblazing ideas that facilitate growth. A myriad of possibilities emerges from under your steely gaze.

It is a landmark time to head towards growth and productivity. Life is ripe with potential; you plant a seed that soon blossoms into a path worth growing as things fall into place. It draws a busy chapter as new options arrive that bring a faster-moving pace. Plotting your goals lets you step towards progressing your career path. You turn a corner and reach a new chapter of possibility.

The Full Moon in Capricorn is the second Supermoon for this year. Notable changes ahead highlight a path towards expanding your social life. A bond blossoms that draws peace and harmony into your life. Emotional awareness guides a fresh start that releases heaviness and removes outworn layers that limit progress. It creates space to focus on a situation that inspires your mind. It teams you up with a friend who brings a saving grace into your foundations that is the giver of renewal and joy. A wave of fresh potential ahead draws rejuvenation. It reboots your foundations and lets you begin building your life blocks per the person you are becoming. Your situation is currently changing and evolving. As you settle into a new normal, you discover growth arrives in curious ways. It begins a quest of working with your abilities and advancing your life into new areas.

Life picks up the pace, and as you gain momentum, a whirlwind of activity tempts you forward. It underscores an atmosphere of abundance that draws balance into your world. It speaks of improvements flowing into your life that connect you with others who support your growth. It sparks a time of sharing thoughts and ideas as you connect with friends. The scene is social, discussions animated, and the pace is lively. Exciting opportunities to mingle with companions are ready to roll into your life. It touches you down with catching up with kindred spirits.

This week speaks of sunshine after rain. It's time to turn your dreams into reality. It opens to a new role that draws benefits into your career path. You plant intentions that let you score an avenue of growth and prosperity. Effectively channeling your energy becomes a turning point that offers room to grow your skills. You make progress on all levels, personal and professional. It helps you move out of your everyday routine as you enjoy an enchanting chapter of progress.

You connect with an opportunity that soon becomes a unique project that offers pleasing results. It does begin a path of increasing chances as you emerge from hibernation, ready to spread your wings. Success is looming as a breakthrough is within reach. It gets you a social aspect that puts you in touch with friends, colleagues, and companions. It brings a social environment that is music to your ears as you touch on expanding your world. You embark on a bold chapter that propels new goals forward. It lets you build a life in an efficient, rewarding manner.

New leads bring an influx of possibilities that opens the floodgates to an enterprising chapter. Creativity and confidence are heightening, leaving you feeling encouraged to try learning new areas. Broadening your horizons lets you explore leads that offer room to grow and flourish. It marks an inspiring time that enables you to move ahead on a clearly defined mission. A venture you become involved with lights a path towards success.

New Moon in Leo and the Delta Aquarids Meteor Shower sees change surrounds your social life and orients you towards expansion. Staying open to new possibilities brings a busy social engagement time that draws a companion to your side. Sharing thoughts and ideas with this person lighten the load as it delivers a wellspring of abundance. You reawaken to the rich landscape of potential as you lift the lid on a chapter that enriches your world.

Information ahead connects you with a chapter of fun and adventure. It brings a time that brims with potential as you scope out a path that offers room to engage with life. Channeling your creative energy into an area that resonates with possibility sees fortune turning in your favor. It takes you on a journey that offers growth, learning, and advancement. It offers a busy and active chapter that draws lively discussions and stimulating conversations with kindred spirits. You set off on a personal mission that brings change and progression.

A welcome piece of news arrives that offers an exciting possibility. As you stand on the precipice of change, you discover new options that encourage expansion in your social life. It lets you turn towards a chapter that highlights abundance, bringing the music flowing sweetly into your world. A happy chapter ahead ushers in new energy. Past struggles fade away as you create a fresh start in a meaningful area. Life picks up steam, and there is plenty of good fortune that brings a boost.

AUGUST

Sun	Mon	Tue	Wed	Thu	Fri	Sat
	1	2	3	4	5	6
7	8	9	10	11	12	13
14	15	16	17	18	19	20
21	22	23	24	25	26	27
28	29	30	31			

August 5th - First Quarter Moon Scorpio 11:06

August 8th - Full Moon in Aquarius Supermoon 01:35. Sturgeon Moon.

August 8th - Perseids Meteor Shower July 17th - August 24th

August 14th - Saturn at Opposition

August 19th - Last Quarter Moon in Taurus 04:36

August 27th - New Moon in Virgo 08:16

August 27th - Mercury at Greatest Eastern Elongation at 27.3 degrees from the Sun

FULL MOON

News arrives that draws a positive influence. It heightens your ability to develop your talents and extend your reach into new areas. Indeed, long-term goals come into focus, essential planning tackles strategy and lets you plot a course towards expansion. It draws an active time that opens your life to a bounty of potential. A new flow of options brings an influx of information. It can take time to process and digest the possibilities. One lead, in particular, sparks your interest, and this marks a turning point that sees you head towards growth and prosperity. It brings a path that is a saving grace as it helps you grow your world in a new direction. It gives you a chance to step up and develop an area that grows your abilities.

The wheel turns in your favor, and it brings a journey forward. It lets you move into new territory that offers learning and growth along the way. It draws movement and discovery. Life heads to an upswing; it brings an active and dynamic environment. Little stands in your way between your vision and reaching your chosen destination. You blaze through a chapter that aligns with creativity. It brings options to be more self-expressive, joyful, and visionary. It enables you to channel your energy higher. As the magic of manifestation courses through your life, you reveal an enticing journey forward.

Full Moon in Aquarius Supermoon and the Perseids Meteor Shower this week brings words of wisdom and guidance that light an enterprising path ahead. It brings information that shifts direction and brings excitement. It pushes back boundaries and lets you move out of your comfort zone and enjoy an active time of social engagement. Sharing ideas, thoughts, and discussions with your broader social circle helps you discover new information. You gently land in an enriching environment that offers support. A time of relaxation connects you with friends, and this rejuvenates and restores equilibrium. It brings possibilities to light that offers advancement.

It expands your life and offers room to share soul-affirming conversations. It kickstarts a beautiful journey of nurturing interpersonal ties. It brings a closer bond that lets you build a stable foundation. Sharing time and experiences with this person becomes a gateway forward. It draws a high note to your social life that enables you to make notable tracks on improving your situation. It is a pivotal time that opens your heart, mind, and spirit to new experiences that offer growth. It gets you connected with a lighter and more fun side of life. It reunites you with what you treasure most, engaging conversations and nurturing bonds that hold meaning. A little worn path calls your name, tempting you forward.

There is increased stability in options that arrive soon. Indeed, positive aspects are ready to flow into your life. Indeed, it's best to streamline the path ahead by letting go of areas that failed to reach fruition. Life becomes rosier as you draw new prospects into your world that revitalize your spirit. It is a time of moving towards new projects and endeavors that capitalize on your talents. It teams you up with other enterprising people, which places you in the box seat to expand your social life. It's a time ripe with potential. Indeed, you can accomplish a great deal by being open to new people and situations. It draws harmony and highlights expansion occurring in your social life. It brings a busy time that offers pathways towards growth.

A new possibility creates a stir of excitement. It reveals information that lets you plot a course towards developing a curious venture. It bestows blessing and opens your life to new pathways. A time of heightening creativity and expansion enables you to tackle an ambitious project. Life becomes busy, giving you the proper nourishment to spread your wings and map out new goals. As you create the stepping stones forward, you maintain stable foundations and draw security into your home life. Its positive influence flows into your world, offering grace and harmony.

In Virgo this week, New Moon combined with Mercury at Greatest Eastern Elongation from the Sun to heighten potential. A lead worth investigating brings a new option to light. It links you up to a chapter that grows your confidence as it gets a unique possibility to light. Your career path heats up when sudden developments arrive to shake up the potential possible. It draws advancement and change that has the potential to reinvent your situation. The time is right for chasing dreams and embracing a journey of growth and prosperity. After the destabilizing times of recent months, you find your feet in a landscape ripe for progression. It helps initiate a positive chapter that carries you forward.

Dramatic change ahead improves your environment as prize news looms overhead. It draws an opportunity that lets you climb the ladder towards success. Connecting with inspiration, you weed out the distractions and streamline your environment to obtain the highest result. New options grow your experience when you cast light upon your career path. Sifting and sorting through possibilities reveals a journey that offers a new role. Acting on instincts lets you embark on a progressive phase that gains momentum and draws an active time of working with your talents.

SEPTEMBER

Sun	Mon	Tue	Wed	Thu	Fri	Sat
				1	2	3
4	5	6	7	8	9	10
11	12	13	14	15	16	17
18	19	20	21	22	23	24
25	26	27	28	29	30	

September 7th - First Quarter Moon Sagittarius 18:08

September 10th - Mercury Retrograde begins in Libra

September 10th - Corn Moon. Harvest Moon. Full Moon in Pisces 09:58

September 16th - Neptune at Opposition

September 17th - Last Quarter Moon in Gemini 21:52

September 23rd - Mabon/Fall Equinox. 01:03

September 25th - New Moon in Libra 21:54

September 26th - Jupiter at Opposition

FULL MOON

You are ready to usher in a new journey. Life holds a curious twist that draws change that leads to advancement. You navigate a path towards growing your abilities. It brings an impressive time of pushing back limitations to reach a chosen destination. Funneling your excess energy into working with your abilities draws a pleasing result. It unearths new options for your career path, and it also connects you with like-minded people who offer wisdom and advice. It speaks of a breakthrough that rains fresh potential down upon your life. It creates space to focus on nurturing your gifts. As you shake off any heavy vibrations that have clung to your energy, you cleanse your spirit, and this releases the tension. It creates space for a fresh chapter of exciting possibilities. You set sail on a journey of a lifetime and soon enter smoother waters. As you gain a better sense of these expanding horizons, you can see options ahead that speak clearly to your spirit. It brings an incredible time of following your vision.

A time of social engagement ahead brings fantastic opportunities to mingle. It draws transformation, and amid a lively and active environment, you discover you can truly thrive. Changes in the air, a fresh wind of potential arrives to bring the gift of connection and abundance. Nurturing friendships with companions brings a joyful chapter into focus. It does cast a light on the social potential that tempts you forward.

Mercury Retrograde begins in Libra. Harvest Moon. Full Moon in Pisces Being flexible and resilient holds you in good stead as you await further information. News arrives that cracks the code to a viable solution. You discover a secret that gives you greater insight into the path ahead. A delicate touch helps you deftly navigate an uncertain time.

Things soon blow over, and the dust settles, bringing grounded energy. But by going over progress, you see nuances that offer room to improve productivity. A decision or action ahead lets you cut away from negativity; it puts you in sync with new possibilities that draw harmony and a lighter chapter. Indeed, an outstanding chapter of growth helps you express talents effectively.

You make notable tracks on improving your situation. A transition ahead shines a light on a viable path that helps you move forward. It brings a grounded time that keeps life progressing towards new options. It brings positive momentum that extends your reach into an area worth growing. After some soul-searching, you get involved with developing your skills, refining your talents draws expansion. An insightful person offers advice to assist your personal growth.

If feeling stuck in a holding pattern, new opportunities soon loom overhead. It brings forth good movement that expands your options. A more prosperous life experience emerges. It lets you grow your world into new areas. Exploring leads allow you to come out a winner as it correlates with expansion and an enterprising path forward. Curious changes ahead signifying a turning point is occurring that smacks of groundbreaking potential.

The future looks rosy. It gets you on course to develop your abilities and expand your skillset into new areas. Amplifying your talents nurtures creativity. It brings a high note into your life that sets the tone for developing new goals and progression areas. Life becomes lighter and sweeter as you step out towards breaking new ground. Little breaks the stride as you enter an enterprising chapter ahead.

You can create headway on achieving new growth by expanding horizons and pushing back boundaries that limit progress. It connects you to a path that draws learning, which helps you make the most of your talents. You discover an adventurous and rustic landscape; it connects you with a broader range of diversity. It brings new companions into your social circle that creates pure magic. You enter a jampacked chapter of refreshing options that grow your world. It brings advancement that leads to a new role.

Mabon/Fall Equinox. New Moon in Libra. Jupiter at Opposition plus a Mercury retrograde in effect causes issues that create mayhem in your social life, and this disruption does take time to resolve. You discover news that tempts you forward. It leads to an extended time of enriching conversations that bring a lift into your life. Setting intentions creates a positive mind space that helps you stay optimistic during an unsettling time navigating into the unknown. You are on the right track to nurturing an environment that bridges the gap towards a brighter future. It draws positive results that help you adeptly navigate complex environments as you move forward with improving the foundations in your home life. You fling open the window to a fresh start and enjoy sunny skies overhead. More open communication lifts the heaviness and rejuvenates foundations.

News arrives soon, which brings a snap decision. Exciting changes sweep into your life and smooth out what has been a bumpy ride. It brings opportunities for growth that let you tackle an inspiring area. It brings a fertile environment from which to grow your life. Life picks up steam, opening your world to new flavors and possibilities. It draws security and provides the grounded platform in which to thrive.

OCTOBER

Sun	Mon	Tue	Wed	Thu	Fri	Sat
						1
2	3	4	5	6	7	8
9	10	11	12	13	14	15
16	17	18	19	20	21	22
23	24	25	26	27	28	29
30	31					

October 2nd - Mercury Retrograde ends in Virgo

October 3rd - First Quarter Moon in Capricorn 00.14

October 7th - Draconids Meteor Shower. Oct 6th -10th

October 8th - Mercury Greatest Western Elongation

October 9th - Hunters Moon. Full Moon in Aries 20:54

October 17th - Last Quarter Moon in Cancer 17.15

October 21st -Orionids Meteor Shower. October 2nd - November 7th

October 25th - New Moon in Scorpio 10:48

October 25th - Partial Solar Eclipse

NEW MOON

FULL MOON

Mercury Retrograde ends in Virgo. Troublesome energy is ready to be released, creating space to heal heralds a fresh start. You head towards a chapter that favors growth; a crossroads ahead brings a decision that lets you cut away from limitations. Potency is brewing that brings a creative element that offers a bridge towards a brighter future. Improvements are coming to your social life; it draws lively discussions and a chance of collaboration. It does let you balance your expectations with options that offer room to grow your world. It sets the tone for developing foundations that enrich your life.

Improvement is ready to flow into your life as a connection with a loved one becomes closer. It heightens the rhythm and pace of your personal life. Flexibility and compassion draw understanding and depth to this union. News arrives that clears the clouds away as it brings sunnier skies overhead. It does see a golden exchange trigger a meaningful moment that gets you back on track with this person. A focus on harmony draws stability and balance into your home life. It orients you towards a wellspring of new possibilities that nurture a situation close to your heart.

A situation you nurture begins to blossom and turn a corner towards smooth sailing. It increases optimism as your life improves, letting you reshape goals and plot a course towards new options.

A Full Moon in Aries shows significant changes are on the horizon. It does bring a trajectory that expands the potential in your world. You plot a course towards your vision and can embrace new possibilities that nurture your talents. Something special is ready to make a grand entrance. It does bring you joy, abundance, and a sense of connection with someone who inspires your mind. All in, you can look forward to a productive and active environment ahead.

Opportunities to socialize are coming soon. It takes you on a journey that gets you in touch with friends and acquaintances. It offers a chance to mingle as you get involved with heightened social and community options. An invitation ahead provides an opportunity to collaborate with another. It brings stability to your life. Your social life is vibrant, and this connects you to secure and grounded foundations.

It speaks about a positive breakthrough or realization that alters your perspective. It lets you spot a window of opportunity that is opening. It does bring options you can pursue with passion. Breaking free of limitations brings positive change. You have a remarkable ability to unearth new possibilities. It brings a chapter that harnesses your creativity to a stellar effect. As your vision broadens, you gain access to unique options that bring growth and prosperity. It brings a marked improvement that emphasizes more security and abundance flowing into your world. As you reawaken to the potential that seeks to enter your life, it empowers your spirit and heals your soul.

It is a time that grows your world. It speaks of new options arriving soon. It brings an active phase that lets you focus on creating positive change. Exploring a wider world of potential sees you turning a corner and heading towards growth. Your willingness to persevere and unearth new possibilities does bring a rewarding chapter where you begin to see your vision taking shape. It lets you reawaken to the magic that is possible in your life.

You have a resilient and robust spirit that overcomes obstacles and navigates around hurdles as needed. It brings the ability to sort out the path ahead and choose one that draws dividends. It is the start of a heightening opportunity that puts a spotlight on freedom and expansion. It revolutionizes the potential possible and delivers a lovely outcome. You see improvements that bring the sparkle back into your world.

Several enticing options cross your path. It does begin a process of developing goals that speak to your heart. New information arrives that opens a compelling road forward. It does see a cycle of reinvention and rejuvenation is taking your focus towards a new level of advancement. You can break free of constraints and dive into uncharted territory. Your willingness to explore new modalities draws dividends. Life becomes rosier as you draw prospects that enliven and inspire your mind. It is a time of moving forward towards developing creative projects.

New Moon in Scorpio with a Partial Solar Eclipse this week. You are ready for the changes ahead. It does see life is about to get exciting; your willingness to explore new options brings rewards. It does illuminate a path forward. It is a time of movement and discovery; you move away from a stale and outworn area and can now reach for new horizons. It does bring an energizing aspect that illuminates a path forward towards a lofty goal.

A new chapter is arriving that brings stable foundations for your personal life. It does create space to nurture a bond that shows promise. It helps you shut the door on a painful chapter. It has you forging ahead towards long-term goals. Discovering the proper outlet for your excess energy brings a bond that enriches and offers room for progression. It does draw a busy and active time; abundance is ready to flow into your life.

Being mindful of your goals lets you create a path that draws abundance. You expand your horizons and enter an auspicious chapter that is creative and bursting with new potential. Life becomes a blaze of activity and adventure. There are some attractive opportunities ahead to inspire your mind. It underscores the energy of magic that surrounds your world. Your willingness to unearth new possibilities draws dividends. It has you landing softly in an expansive environment that pushes back the boundaries. New Horizons tempt you forward.

NOVEMBER

Sun	Mon	Tue	Wed	Thu	Fri	Sat
		1	2	3	4	5
6	7	8	9	10	11	12
13	14	15	16	17	18	19
20	21	22	23	24	25	26
27	28	29	30			

November 1st - First Quarter Moon in Aquarius 06.37

November 4th - Taurids Meteor Shower. September 7th - December 10th

November 8th - Full Moon in Taurus 11:01 Beaver Moon. November 8th - Total Lunar Eclipse

November 9th - Uranus at Opposition

November 16th - Last Quarter Moon in Leo 13:27

November 17th - Leonids Meteor Shower Nov 6th-30th

November 23rd - New Moon in Sagittarius 22:57

November 30th - First Quarter Moon Pisces 14:36

FULL MOON

Taurids Meteor Shower brings harmony and abundance flow into your world to inspire your mind. It brings possibilities that activate a creative phase. It teams you up with a path that offers you room to grow your talents. Soon enough, you connect with others of a similar mindset. It sparks a chapter of sharing thoughts and connecting with friends and companions. It brings an opportunity to head out into a community environment with kindred spirits.

Change is in the air. It has you dreaming about the possibilities when surprise news lands on your doorstep. It brings a new lead from which to progress your world. Paying attention to signs and serendipity also helps guide your path towards increasing prosperity. You can obtain a solid foundation from which to grow your world. It marks a highly productive chapter that becomes a source of inspiration. It shines brightly in your life. News arrives that bestows blessings. It is a time of good fortune and luck that brings new pathways to explore. It rules the time of creativity to tackle ambitious projects that offer room to grow your skills and abilities. It marks a unique path, and changing conditions bring new possibilities to light. You reach a turning point that takes your aspirations further. It lands you in an environment that is ripe with potential. There is an emphasis on initiating new projects and endeavors.

Full Moon in Taurus. Total Lunar Eclipse speaks of a path that draws abundance. You can permit yourself to follow your heart, chase your dreams, and know that you are on a continuous cycle of growth, evolution, and change.

A more social environment does have you mingling with new people. There are rewards to be found by being open to new experiences. It starts a chapter that offers remarkable growth in your life. It does light a path towards an abundant chapter that brings bright possibilities into your life. You can take advantage of opportunities to network with others.

You are progressing forward; being mindful of your goals keeps your work focused, which draws dividends. A group endeavor ahead brings an opportunity that offers room to grow your skills. It connects you with others who seek a similar destination. It brings a time of pushing back boundaries and challenging yourself with growth and learning. News arrives that shifts your focus to a unique possibility.

Enchanting information arrives that promotes harmony. It does seem these news snippets light a new chapter for your social life. It draws lively discussions that inspire personal growth. Motivation arises, and it brings a uniquely uplifting time of exploring the synergy with someone of interest.

Leonids Meteor Shower brings a landmark moment; it is a gateway toward a brighter future. You connect with like-minded people, both online and in person. It gets the ball rolling on improving your social life. It draws a turning point the flings open the doors to a fresh start. Communication, collaboration and joint ventures pave the way forward towards impressive goals. It marks a bold beginning that opens a path towards developing your talents, creativity, and skills. Brainstorming sessions kick off trailblazing ideas.

You can start putting your intentions into action. During this valuable time, shifting into builder mode lets you progress your concepts and create tangible forms of your ideas. The time is ripe for projects and endeavors as you soon kick off a prosperous chapter of initiating new ventures. It is a powerful time for manifesting; an area you get off the ground soon takes shape. You enter a purposeful time of using your talents to achieve pleasing results. Performance is rising, drawing accolades and success.

You benefit from new opportunities that take you towards a refreshing chapter. Creativity is rising, and this encourages growth and learning. If you have felt as though you are standing at the crossroads, a decision you make turns out to be a winner.

New Moon in Sagittarius You enter an energizing time that hits a high note; it opens a path that reveals new information. It is a time that draws change and brings an option that advances your situation forward. A new adventure comes calling and blossoms into an exciting path forward. As you navigate the stepping stones towards success, it sets the tone for an inspiring time of chasing your vision. It leads to an expressive environment that draws a rewarding social aspect. It casts light upon an area that nurtures growth and well-being. You unleash possibilities that kick off a stable phase of advancement. It draws security that lays the correct foundation for your home life. Provides a secure link that helps you forge a unique path ahead.

Unexpected news materializes before your eyes, and it's a beauty. It brings a journey that offers a busy time filled with the promise of expansion. It opens the door to luck and optimism. It brings lively discussions and the sharing of thoughts and ideas with another. Spending time with a valued companion nurtures abundance and draws harmony into your world. It lights up pathways of creativity and social engagement that draw balance into your life. Heartwarming progress brings a boost that offers impressive results for your social life.

DECEMBER

Sun	Mon	Tue	Wed	Thu	Fri	Sat
				1	2	3
4	5	6	7	8	9	10
11	12	13	14	15	16	17
18	19	20	21	22	23	24
25	26	27	28	29	30	31

December 8th - Cold Moon. Moon Before Yule
December 8th - Full Moon in Gemini 04:07
December 8th - Mars at Opposition

December 13th - Geminids Meteor Shower. Dec 7th- 17th

December 16th - Last Quarter Moon in Virgo 08:56

December 21st - Ursids Meteor Shower December 17 - 25th December 21 - Mercury at Greatest Eastern elongation.
December 21st - Yule/Winter Solstice at 09:48

December 23rd - New Moon in Capricorn 10:16

December 29th - Mercury Retrograde begins in Capricorn

December 30th - First Quarter Moon Aries 01:21

FULL MOON

You've been through an unpredictable time recently, but there is exciting potential brewing in your life's background. It makes itself known soon and clears the slate for a fresh chapter. Information arrives that shakes up the potential. It invigorates your spirit and offers an opportunity for growth. Incorporating this news into your plans is a pivotal moment. It unleashes your talents in an area ripe for progression. Exploring leads soon lets you head towards a direction that draws stable foundations. It allows you to reach for something more, and you soon enter an extended time of developing goals.

News arrives that helps you stay on top of the game in your working life. Many changes are surrounding your industry, and exploring new technologies, places you in the proper alignment to capitalize on your talents. You benefit from a flexible and pragmatic approach as you prepare to embark on a new journey forward. Carefully exploring options lets, you obtain due diligence before embarking on your next chapter of growth.

A friend returns in your life, and this kicks off a chapter of sharing treasured memories. It does bring changes that stabilize foundations. It sees you improving your living situation. This person is intelligent and insightful; they open doors and bring generosity and wisdom to the table. It draws advancement into your home life and triggers an active phase of developing a bond that sparks potential.

Full Moon in Gemini and Mars at Opposition create a curious blend of mystery and mayhem. A social aspect ahead links you up to an intriguing companion. This person has charm, magnetism, and a supportive personality. You are in your element as you touch down on deepening a bond that glimmers with potential. It draws a lucky time that offers surprising intensity as the energy sizzles. It sees you pursuing your dreams with an open heart, and you soon discover the feelings are mutual.

You can set the bar higher and embark on new adventures with unbridled enthusiasm. It brings a time of exploring the possibilities that open the path ahead for your social life. Something new is around the corner in terms of support; it heats a sense of passion and connects you with a kindred spirit. Stimulating growth in your social life sees you moving from strength to strength.

It marks a new beginning that helps you make up for the lost time. It widens the sense of support in your social life. It draws activity that lets you escape into lively conversations with someone who has you feeling excited about the possibilities. Conversations with this companion are energizing; it creates a seedling that, when nurtured, offers tremendous growth. It amplifies emotions and gets you in touch with what you seek. Spending time with a companion adds sparkle to your world.

Ursids Meteor Shower. Mercury at Greatest Eastern elongation. Yule/Winter Solstice at week's end. There are opportunities ahead to nurture a closer bond with loved ones. It brings a time of new inspiration that reawakens creativity. It brings opportunities to unwind with family as it emphasizes sharing time and experiences with those who are meaningful. It draws lengthy conversations that let you head towards a happier chapter. It speaks of a time ahead that rules expansion for your social life. It hits a positive note that expands your life outwardly. Technology plays an integral part in keeping social bonds connected. The warmth of friendship and the anticipation of fun looming overhead brings a happy chapter to light. Warmth and companionship flow into your world, drawing freedom and abundance.

Surprise news arrives that offers a closer friendship with someone who has previously drifted out of your life. It does begin a new chapter that provides expansion and renewal. It draws a relaxing time of sharing news and communication with a person who offers support and advice. A positive influence does wonders for your spirit when a social aspect highlights growth is possible. It brings stable energy that sees a situation evolving and becoming closer. It positions you correctly to develop a journey that draws excitement as it touches you down in a vibrant landscape of possibility.

New Moon in Capricorn. Mercury Retrograde begins this week. It shows a complex environment that can drain your spirit. Overthinking, feeling restless can create disruptions that cause issues. Scaling back some of your life tasks enables you to focus on anchoring your energy in a grounded environment. Drawing balance and equilibrium restores creative energy.

News arrives that highlights a digital project that offers the chance of social engagement. It brings communication as innovative collaboration springs to life. Making your dreams a priority allows you to heal the past and remove areas that are no longer relevant. It brings a fruitful time of planning your vision for future growth. You pass the threshold and enter a brighter, happier chapter. Important news arrives to tempt you out with friends. Mingling and networking bring a sense of belonging that balances flagging spirits.

Life holds a refreshing change. Exciting changes are coming up. There is a buzz of activity around your social life that brings news, invitations, and events. It is a great time to nurture your personal life. The path ahead shimmers with potential. Lively discussions team you up with a beautiful sense of connection. Constructive dialogues create brainstorming sessions that reveal information that opens a route towards liberation and freedom. Life becomes a blur of active busyness. You create growth and secure solid foundations by harnessing the power of this energy.

Dear Stargazer,

I hope you have enjoyed planning your year with the stars utilizing Astrology and Zodiac influences. My yearly zodiac books feature a weekly (four weeks to a month) horoscope. You can find me on the sites below, where you can get personal astrology or intuitive readings.

https://www.facebook.com/SiaSands

Instagram: SiaSands

You can order an Astrology reading at:

https://psychic-emails.com/

Leaving a review is welcomed and appreciated.

Many Blessings,

Sia Sands

Printed in Great Britain
by Amazon

86679187R00068